The Top End

A Celebration of Australia's

Top End

Perched at the northern tip of the Australian continent is the extreme and spectacular wilderness of the Top End. For much of the year the scorched sandstone ridges of the Arnhem Land escarpment rise, as bare as bones, from the dry earth; however, during wet season, a lush tropical paradise flourishes, resplendent with cascading waterfalls and abundant with plant and animal life. Amid the breathtaking beauty of nature sits Darwin, Australia's northernmost capital and a city that has risen from cyclonic destruction to become a modern, multicultural hub for the Top End's remote areas.

As well as being a naturalist's paradise, the Top End is ancient Australia at its most glorious. Here the Aboriginal people of Kakadu and surrounding areas celebrate over 60,000 years of culture, preserving rock art and maintaining a deep spiritual connection with this land. I hope you feel the remarkable spirit of these people and of this rugged region when you journey through this book.

Steve Parish

6–25   DARWIN

26–47   A WETLAND WONDER WORLD

48–79   STONE COUNTRY

80–95   WOODLANDS & FORESTS

Left to right: Each year, Darwinians dress up and celebrate the Top End's eclectic ethnic mix at the colourful Darwin Festival, which includes a grand parade featuring cultural dress, dancing, and a smorgasbord of food from all corners of the globe.

 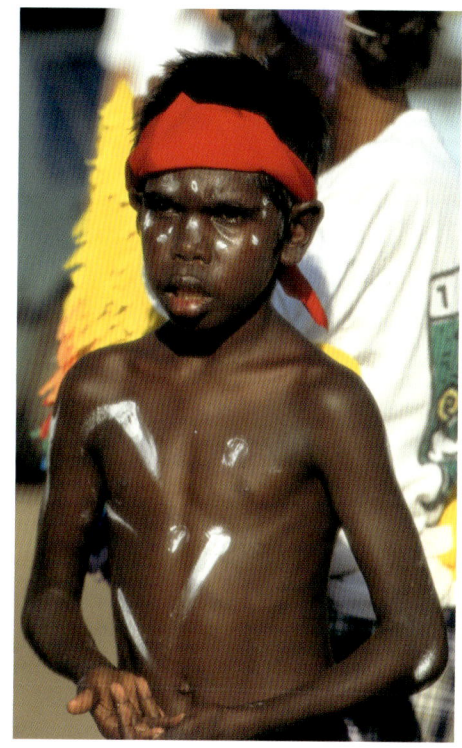

Above: Arnhem Land escarpment; an Aboriginal boy joins the festivities.

A modern, *multicultural* city poised amid an ancient paradise.

Drovers lead cattle along the stock routes, stirring dust from the trails and pressing their stockhorses onwards in the quest for greener pastures.

A young girl enjoys her solitude, near Victoria River.

Isolation is a way of life for this carefree cyclist.

Far-flung, *isolated* residents use their remote capital as a meeting place of minds and a service centre for city comforts.

The balmy climate entices swimmers into the patrolled waters of Mindil Beach.

Outdoors-loving citizens grasp every opportunity to *celebrate*

Top left: The Top End's unique Daly Waters Hotel. Bottom left: Colourful street markets are a social event. Right: A rare role reversal — humans feed fish in Darwin. Both locals and visitors enjoy the more unusual activity of feeding barramundi, bream, milkfish and other fish species by hand at Aquascene in Doctors Gully, right in the heart of the city.

Darwin's coast is vermilion

at *sunset*

and kissed by aquamarine waters by day.

Sunset bestows a cool peace to a hot city.

Dusk softens the jagged edges of rocks at Nightcliff.

Darwin city, seen from the air, nestles amid a tropical paradise of azure and emerald.

Locals and visitors alike embrace the *cooling* sea breezes that breathe life into long days in the tropics.

Salt-encrusted hollows in wave-worn tidal outcrops, and tangles of stunted mangroves, are home to many marine treasures.

Easily accessible beaches lure locals to Fannie Bay (above) and the Timor Sea coast (above centre).

In Litchfield National Park, cascading waters flow into cool pools at Buley Rockhole — a haven from the heat.

To stave off the unrelenting sun,
a life-giving rush of *water* tumbles from ancient,
craggy gorges...

A toddler delights in a fountain in Darwin Mall.

Spectacular Florence Falls stream into a deep, refreshingly cold basin.

Above: Aborigines, such as this boy Tumbo, have refreshed themselves at Florence Falls for centuries.
Opposite: Wangi Falls sluice over weathered rock in Litchfield National Park and create another popular cooling-off point for visitors.

Crystal-clear *cascades* gather momentum on the plateaus and peaks then pour their ice-cold torrents into rocky chasms.

Crocodiles and humans *cohabit* warily around the shared, mangrove-fringed waterways of the Top End.

Powerful, prehistoric Estuarine Crocodiles are revered in Indigenous culture and are totemic for this territory, where locals have learned to live with and accept their presence.

Adding a Top End twist to the boxing kangaroo is the boxing "croc" at Humpty Doo.

A Wetland Wonder World

Sun-dappled surfaces cover an incredible, interwoven ecosystem...

Clouds fleet across the mirrored magnificence of a lily-filled waterhole at the Territory Wildlife Park.

Top and above: Liquid light shimmering in Kakadu National Park.

Brilliance *gleams* from the shining, mirrored surfaces of this remarkable watery habitat.

A moment of reflection in a Jacana's graceful flight from a Kakadu billabong.

Yellow Water, a refuge for wading birds and freshwater life in World Heritage-listed Kakadu National Park.

Drenching wet season *floods* promise renewed life, filling the billabongs and urging a burst of lush life.

Clockwise from top left: Freshwater fish flourish, including Sleepy Cod; Male and female Purple-spotted Gudgeons; Eel-tailed Catfish; Seven-spot Archerfish; Chequered Rainbowfish; Saratoga.

Barramundi — perhaps the best-known Top End fish.

The Pig-nosed Turtle is the only freshwater turtle to have large flippers like those of a marine turtle.

Below the sparkling surface *glide* equally shining fishes and patient, rapacious reptiles.

Estuarine Crocodiles, also known as Saltwater Crocodiles, are masters of camouflage, often floating near the surface with just their eyes and nostrils exposed.

Little Grebe

Watch for canny carnivores *lurking* in the warm waters.

An exquisite crown of pastel *lilies* tops these fertile waters.

Above and opposite: Water lilies rise from the mirrored billabongs like regal, floral sceptres.

Wetland serenity is disturbed only by rings of gentle ripples and the soft shush of *wings* gliding over this avian airstrip.

Clockwise from left: The Magpie Goose, one of the Top End's most common waterbirds; Pied Cormorant; Plumed Whistling-Duck; Comb-crested Jacana.

Clockwise from left: A wading bird paradise — Brolgas; Jabiru or Black-necked Stork; a Jabiru and egrets in silhouette; Royal Spoonbills.

Anbangbang Billabong is filled with monsoonal rain that runs off the towering sandstone outcrop of Nourlangie Rock, Kakadu National Park.

Sunset fades in a gradient of *dusky* hues then slips between darkened trees.

Above and opposite: Australian Pelicans scour the still waters for a feast of fish below.

Stone Country

Crags and chasms are moody features on

the face of this country carved from stone...

Dramatic sandstone cliffs plummet from the spine of the Arnhem Land escarpment in Kakadu National Park.

"*...from one of the hills which bounded its narrow valley, I had a most disheartening, sickening view over a tremendously rocky country. A high land composed of horizontal strata of sandstone, seemed to be literally hashed, leaving the remaining blocks in fantastic figures of every shape...*"
Ludwig Leichhardt, 11 November 1844

Like abstract sculptures of Nature, these stone "mushrooms" stand at Ubirr.

Plunging cliffs of the Arnhem Land escarpment, Kakadu National Park.

Jim Jim Falls roar into full flood when swollen with wet season rains in Kakadu National Park.

The pounding pressure of Twin Falls in flood kneads the rocks at the fall's base in Kakadu National Park.

Rushing *torrents* tear at the rock, eroding valuable nutrients with which to wash and fertilise the floodplains.

For many millennia, fast-flowing streams during the wet season have sculpted the stone and replenished the water supply for animals such as this Mertens' Water Monitor.

Raging waters score the rock and create a veil of cascades at Jim Jim Falls, Kakadu National Park.

The blue horizon is pierced by *jagged* fortresses of sandstone, ringed by trees.

The landscape of Kakadu National Park is an architecture of stony towers, stacks, mountains and caves, many with special significance to Aboriginal people.

Boulders balance awkwardly at Ubirr, Kakadu National Park — the result of the surrounding rock eroding over the aeons.

Above and opposite: The Nardab Floodplains recline before Ubirr Lookout in Kakadu National Park — an area of great significance to Aborigines and a major tourist attraction.

From Ubirr, the *vista* sweeps over tracts of trees and passages of time, to days of dreaming...

Even the rocks have long memories and recount ancient tales in *galleries* of Aboriginal culture.

Above: Anbangbang Gallery, on the canvas of Nourlangie Rock, records more than 20,000 years of Aboriginal culture. Left: Depictions of Aboriginal Creation Ancestors, including Namondjok (top left) and Namarrgon (top right) — the Lightning Man who crashes stone axes together to make thunder and lightning.

A rock-art portrait of the endemic Oenpelli Python.

Aboriginal *art* is truly a beautiful depiction of life and beliefs...

Barramundi have been a significant food source for Aborigines for centuries.

The fat-rich meat of the Northern Long-necked Turtle is a traditional and highly prized Aboriginal food source.

Large flippers and a distinctive, porcine nose distinguish this artwork as an unmistakable impression of the Pig-nosed Turtle.

Above and right: The great chimney stacks of sandstone that rise from the Lost City, near the Nathan River and the Tawallah Range in Litchfield National Park, are unique landforms that are largely inaccessible.

Above and opposite: Nitmiluk National Park is scored by the deep fissure of Katherine Gorge and the snaking Katherine River.

Above: Tour cruises take in the splendour of the Katherine River and Gorge in Nitmiluk National Park.
Right: The Katherine River flows through Katherine Gorge.

Thirteen spectacular gorges are secreted in Nitmiluk National Park, many are accessible only by canoe.

Life appears to rise from the *depths* of this winding, sapphire chasm fringed with grateful green...

Cracks and crevices *shelter* wildlife from the secretive to the sublimely vivid.

Clockwise from left: Leichhardt's Grasshopper; Sandstone Frog; Giant Cave Gecko; Prickly Knob-tailed Gecko

A Rock Ringtail Possum shyly peers from its safe haven on a rocky ledge.

Short-eared Rock-wallabies inhabit a Top End range from the Western Australian Kimberley around to the Gulf of Carpentaria in Queensland.

The timid and rarely seen Black Wallaroo is only found along the western edge of the Arnhem Land escarpment.

Through fire, flood and famine the forest endures, responding with a flourish of growth...

Tall grasses become brittle kindling during the dry season, broken only by occasional green plants.

Clockwise from left: Green Ants; Black-headed Python; grasshoppers; Lesser Wanderer Butterfly.

Tiny insects, vibrant butterflies, opportunistic reptiles
— all keep their *secrets* here.

By night, the darkness *rustles*

and dapples with shadows of swiftly moving life.

Clockwise from top left: Tornier's Frog; juvenile Common Ringtail Possum; Desert Death Adder; Common Rock Rat — all inhabitants of the tropical Top End's woodlands and forests. Left: Northern Brown Bandicoot.

Commonly seen in Top End waterholes, the Jabiru or Black-necked Stork is the continent's only stork species.

Birds *swoop* in to wetland paperbarks and dabble for fish near submerged roots in the tea-coloured waters.

Tree roots create hidey-holes for invertebrates. Raindrops glisten on leaves and fill waterways. Fallen trees and leaves provide perches and cover.

Above, left to right: Elegance in flight — an Osprey swoops down towards its chick; White-bellied Sea-Eagle.

Azure Kingfishers add a vivid flash of colour.

A small, shy Lemon-bellied Flycatcher finds a quiet perch in the freshwater mangroves.

For the male Great Bowerbird, courtship requires a headress of vivid, mauve-pink nape feathers and the construction of an elaborate bower.

Birds bring *vibrancy* to the more muted tones of twig, leaf and branch.

Above left: A Red-winged Parrot grooms its crimson and emerald plumage.
Above right: The aptly named Rainbow Lorikeet.

Dawn creeps stealthily into the dank darkness of the paperbark forest, illuminating tree trunks and evaporating morning mist.

In Aboriginal legend, *Gundaman*, the Frilled Lizard, was once a man; he was turned into the scaly, frilled reptile by elders when he was inattentive during rituals.

Courageous and *dramatic* the Frilled Lizard is a master in the art of bluffing.

Published by Steve Parish Publishing Pty Ltd
PO Box 1058, Archerfield, Queensland 4108 Australia
© copyright Steve Parish Publishing Pty Ltd
All rights reserved. No part of this publication may be reproduced, stored in a retrieval system, or transmitted in any form or by any means, electronic, mechanical, photocopying, recording or otherwise, without the prior permission in writing of the publisher.
ISBN 9781741932225
First published 2007. Reprinted 2008.
Photography: Steve Parish
Additional photography: Ian Morris: pp. 24 (left), 25 (bottom), 40 (centre bottom), 56 (bottom left), 65, 76 (left & centre top), 77–79, 83 (centre bottom & right), 84–85 & 90; Michael Cermak: pp. 36–37.
Front cover: Nourlangie Rock, Kakadu National Park. Title page: A cane sculpture of a boat on Mindil Beach, Darwin. Pages 2–3: Sunset over one of Darwin's beaches. Pages 6–7: The tide floods mangroves on Darwin's coast. Pages 26–27: The sun reflected in a Top End billabong. Pages 36–37: Freshwater Crocodile basking. Pages 48–49: Nourlangie Rock and surrounding sandstone features, Kakadu National Park. Pages 80–81: Pandanus trees in Top End woodland.
Text: Karin Cox, SPP
Design: Gill Stack, SPP
Editorial: Britt Winter, Ted Lewis
Production: Carol Chandler; Jacqueline Schneider, SPP
Prepress by Colour Chiefs Digital Imaging, Brisbane, Australia
Printed in China by Printplus Limited

Produced in Australia at the Steve Parish Publishing Studios

Steve Parish PUBLISHING

www.steveparish.com.au
www.photographaustralia.com.au